POETIC JUSTICE

COMPILED AND EDITED BY
Ellen Stackable
Claire Collins
Hanna Al-Jibouri
Maggie Lane
Jenna Jones

POETRY BY
Women at David L. Moss Criminal Justice Center
in Tulsa, Oklahoma

LOGO DESIGN BY
Jonathan Heckman

GRAPHIC DESIGN BY
Jacob Cossey

PHOTOGRAPHY BY
James Gibbard

ISBN 978-1-943842-63-6

POETIC JUSTICE WOULD LIKE TO THANK

Oklahoma Literary Arts Alliance, Sheri Curry, Sgt. Stacie Holloway, the Detention Officers at David L. Moss, Kent Martin, all those who donated funds in order to make this anthology possible, and the hundreds of women who bravely shared these stories from their lives while inside David L. Moss.

INTRODUCTION

We began a year and a half ago with a question and a hope: Could writing poetry transform a person's life, even a person in jail? From this question, Poetic Justice was born.

Poetic Justice is a writing class that addresses two harrowing realities of its community: First, that Oklahoma houses more incarcerated women per capita than any other state in the nation, and in fact doubles the national average of female incarceration. Second, that approximately 80% of the women incarcerated in Oklahoma are being detained for non-violent crimes.

Our class takes place once a week in the temporary home of hundreds of women in Oklahoma: David L. Moss Criminal Justice Center. Within the jail's walls, described by one of Poetic Justice's students as her "Mossy Crossroads," female prisoners are placed in one of three housing divisions called "pods." Each pod contains a small classroom outfitted with a counter, a sink, and a whiteboard.

Week after week, when the jail's operators open the huge steel doors to let us into the pod, we find up to 25 students already sitting in the classroom waiting for us, hoping to guarantee their spot. Most of the women that we meet are mothers, many of them grandmothers. Most champion seen or unseen scars from the many abuses they have endured. These are women who often feel hopeless and voiceless. Poetic Justice journeys with these women as each one discovers within herself her own unique voice. This discovery of their voice equips our students with the hope and the power to change the paths of their lives. For two hours each week our small space is transformed and the women in the class tell us that they feel truly free—free to explore in writing their pasts, to consider their present, and to write of their hopes for the future. Time after time as they read what they have written out loud, we cry and laugh together and feel utterly safe in that most unsafe place.

At the end of our five weeks together, we celebrate the incredible work of our students with a graduation ceremony. Many of our students share that this is their first time graduating from any sort of program. Five weeks ago, some these same women told us that they had never written anything in their lives. We give them graduation certificates and an anthology of their poetry. They are, we tell them, published poets.

This anthology contains the best poems from Poetic Justice's previous eight anthologies. It is compiled from the extraordinary writing of over 400 women. Within its pages you will hear from the heartbreaking, eloquent, and beautiful voices of women who have for years felt voiceless. These poems and letters house a deep trauma, a tentative healing, and a hope for the future.

ATTRIBUTIONS

Poems that begin with "What it's like to be" are after Patricia Smith's poem "What it's Like to be a Black Girl (for those of you who aren't)".

Letters in the anthology are after Lauren Zuniga's poem "Dear Lauren Barry".

Poems that begin with "Here in the…of my life" are after Anne Sexton's "The Room of My Life".

Poems that begin with "what you'd find" are after Francine Harris' poem "what you'd find buried in the dirt under charles f. kettering sr. high school (detroit, michigan).

TABLE *of* CONTENTS

NONINSTITUTIONALIZED

This morning when I woke
I was nothing but a jaded, worn out
childless mother
Awakening to a phantom child's call
I was pent up in more ways than one
Penitent and incomplete.
Feloniously, infamously and truly unique
Heartbroken, despondent, down-trodden and beat
This morning when I woke
I was more than I ever imagined I could be
A daughter divinely favored
Awakening to a near Goddess's call
I was set free on many levels
Unmarred and composed a whole
rhythmically, silently and truly in control
Hopeful, expectant, unconquerable
brimming with soul
This morning when I woke
I was perfectly flawed and beautifully scarred
Awakening to the spirit of my ancient
sub-consciousness call
I was nothing and everything
in every possible way
I was one with the infinite confined to this
bodily temple
An unfinished work
enough to fill a thousand pages
Seeking wisdom from fleeting sages
Sublime and transcending
though held by man's earthly cages.

-O.J.

ODE TO MUSIC

Peace of mind
It's music time
The sounds of R&B
R. Kelly's "Your Body's Calling Me"
I close my eyes, the joy inside, the image in my mind.
Snappin' my fingers/ It's hammer time.
You can't touch this music.
I love, I trust this. Whether I'm feeling happy or sad
Music is good for the soul.
James Brown, "Papa's got a brand new bag."
Boy, I'm old.
From "Thriller" to "Billie Jean"
I love to hear Michael Jackson's voice.
"P.Y.T." Pretty Young Thing
The sun shines outside
Music helps me unwind
My heart beats fast when my favorite song is on,
I'm shakin' my ass, not too much
I'm a lady, not a slut.
Beyonce's "Single Ladies" is the cut.
Music never dies
it goes on for ever and ever
From legends to songwriters
 artists, bands, producers and fans
I'm a lover of music, once it's on
I dance.

-L.J.H

SCARS

He left his scars
They don't show
Imprinted them within my soul,
So forgive me, my friend
If I get scared
But my emotions
Are temporarily
Under repair.

-M.G.Z.

WHAT IT'S LIKE TO BE AN INCARCERATED WIFE AND MOTHER FOR THOSE OF YOU WHO AREN'T

It's waking up to see an array of colors, sleepy faces, unfinished homework on the kitchen table.

It's hearing three toddler boys fighting over crayons, toy cars, video games, and bath time. A baby girl crying for me to feed her.

It's feeling the love in my husband's arms when I'm mad, sad, happy or glad.

It's the taste of restaurant food when he takes me to dinner to celebrate our anniversary that I won't be in attendance for this year...

Waking up to realize I'm surrounded by one hundred women all dressed alike, providing comfort to each other after a disappointing court date, eating bland dinners together.

Some have no one to call, others mad at the ones who betrayed them, although we've all betrayed ourselves...

It's reminding myself I made the decision to do what I did wrong and now I'm the incarcerated wife and mother!

-A.C.

DEAR LONELY PRINCESS

Did you know your name actually means princess? That means always be treated like one no matter how much you love him or her.

Do not be afraid of being alone; even though that fear follows you throughout adulthood.

Don't let it control the smart, beautiful woman you become. Don't get married young or think you know everything. Sweetie, you don't.

Every obstacle, challenge, heartache and struggle you face; you will overcome and become that much stronger.

You are talented so use that to your advantage.

Anything you set your mind to you can achieve.

If you ever meet a man nicknamed 'Wicked', run like hell was set loose and demons want to eat your soul because if you fall into his trap he will be the one to eat it. The abuse is not worth the love the abusers offer you.

You are NOT a monster and will never be one.

You are loved more than you can ever imagine.

Do not change you for anyone or anything and maybe someday you'll realize change is not always bad.

If you ever end up raped and bloody, the baby kicked out of your stomach; if you ever look in the mirror and see a black eye or two, or you look at the person you lay next to and hate them but are scared of being alone, LEAVE.

Do not try to kill yourself or use a substance so you won't feel the bruises he inflicts on you day after day.

NOBODY is worth your soul, sanity or the rest of your life behind bars.

Live life, experiment with women, love, and your hair (it'll always grow back).

Speak your mind.

Fuck everyone else's opinion of you.

You're a fucking princess, own it.

XOXO Love the one and only,

Country the Clown

P.S. You WILL survive, and when he told you forever, it was a lie.

-S.F.

HOW I SIT IN THIS CELL

As I sit in this cell, I think, "Damn, I'm in jail."
It's *real*, not a drill. The way I feel, from drug life
to sober living, realizing it was myself
I was killing.
As I struggle I'm in so much pain
thinking about what I have to gain.
I know in my head this shall pass.
I just don't know how long it will last.
Being locked up and locked down hurts
when the fam ain't around.
Outta sight, outta mind it's how I fill my time.
Where's the support when I go to court?
Nowhere to be found.
God is with me so who can be against me?
The life I live is a struggle. Walk a mile in my shoes. Can you got through what I've
been through? Why me?

-K

DEAR G.E.

Look at you now, skipping school to go get high. Not knowing what the future just might bring. Beating up people and running away, not giving a fuck what Mother had to say. How many nights she stayed up crying, going and going like the bunny they say. Not knowing how dumb and funny you look when you get older. When Aunt Shanna and the girls died it seemed to get worse. You see, I wanted to die. Fuck, I wanted to get high. There was no limit for the cutting, scarring I have on me. Slamming dope and selling it, that's what I wanted for me. Knowing there is so much more to this life. See when Grandma died I did a shot of dope because I didn't wanna feel. There is so much more than what you feel. I do not blame you, nor do I hate you. I love you because of you, you made me who I am. I know my worth and I'll stand for that. I'll make it through more days. I have someone new who cares for me. She's waiting for me now. So what else shall I say to you G.E.? Get it together NOW, before you wake up and they are all gone and you have wasted your whole life.
P.S. Don't skip school and smoke that dope.

-G.E.

WHAT YOU'D FIND IN THE DIRT AT MY DAUGHTER'S HOUSE

Dog shit, and dog hair, cigarette butts; way too many for a house of non-smokers. chew toys and chew bones, spoons left from digging up worms, holes in the ground from digging up the worms, glitter, insulation that the firemen pulled out of the ceiling when the house caught on fire, skateboards, skateboard ramps and rails, footballs, a flat basketball, hair-ties and huge blobs of bubblegum, half eaten cheap lollipop, an orange plastic jack o' lantern, bones, collapsed dirty pool covered in mud and leaves, lawn chairs, left out from a night of watching shooting stars, a list of wishes to wish on shooting stars, more cigarette butts, an empty oil can, a plastic purple easter egg with a clump of melted jelly, a few empty fast food drink cups with pop still in the bottom, two cats; one named Meatball (he has to be the biggest ragdoll cat I've ever seen) and his momma Miss Kitty the bitch. Two Pomeranians; Baby Girl and Yiddle, and Yiddle's waiting rock, where he waits for his momma to come home.

-C.M.

HELPING HANDS

My mind could explode with emotion,
Bleed here with compassion;
Many Women's Wounds may not heal as
I think;
Smothering in loneliness and negativity
fighting to keep afloat
Lord use me to throw them a
floatation device;
I prefer to work in the realm of
God's fruitfulness;
Love
Joy
Peace
Patience
Kindness
Gentleness
Faithfulness
And Self Control
Thank You Lord for mirroring your
Grace through me,
All of them hold immense beauty
together let's show them so they
too can see they're forgiven
they're loved, their
inner beauty.

-L.H.D.

AN ODE TO NOODLES

Noodles for lunch
Noodles for dinner
and yet I wonder why I'm not thinner.
Orange sporks
Plastic bowls
a tummy full of noodles and rolls
Start to grow.
So many choices, yummy they are
Once a medium now an extra-large.
I eat them crunchy
I like them like that
and now when describing me they use the word fat.
I'm thankful for noodles
It's crazy I know,
But late at night they comfort the soul.
What! This beef!? I ordered chili
Arguing over noodles is really quite silly.
I like noodles
I like them a lot
and sometimes in jail it seems all you got.

-L.S.

WHAT IT'S LIKE TO BE ME, THE AMPUTEE
(FOR THOSE OF YOU WHO AREN'T)

What is it like to be the girl with the "leg"?
 People staring your way and pointing fingers.
I can't even begin to imagine what little kids think...
I've had a few run away scared.
Do they think I'm a monster? Or half of a human?
I really don't know. I consider myself whole.
But, I wouldn't want you to have to walk in my shoe.
It still bothers me to this day.
I've learned to appreciate it in a lot of ways.
"It's just a limb Miesha, you still got your life."
That's what I tell myself,
as the devil tries to keep me down.
I got God and God's got me. I'm the girl, the amputee.
Sometimes I want to take off running, but here I am
still standing in the same place.

-M.M.

THINGS I'VE LEARNED AT DAVID L. MOSS

These few trips have not been easy. All of this was very traumatizing from the beginning, with the crooked cops wrenching me around, tasering me over and over. I tried to save my arm. What would you do? The shower room, that smell of cleaner; the medical waiting room with the urine stench. The medical cells with blood from others. The horrible fumes of this place have me hacking, coughing, vomiting. The mental escapees, dykes, human traffickers, pregnant woman, barely legal girls, drug makers, drug dealers, women seeking recovery, women doing drugs, some selling drugs, escorts, thieves, hot dates, corrupt detention officers, false accusations, bitches hating, commissary hoes, commissary pimpin', D.O.'s in here to meet other women, washer and dryer working over double time. The devil is hard at work, preventing inmates from pulling chain. Temptations, stinking women, cornbread begging inmates, Sheriff, top flight security, taking their jobs to the maximum capabilities. Men who do strange things behind cell doors, calls tapped by laws, everything recorded.

-M.G.

BANKRUPT

I'm poor in zoom zoomz and wam wamz
I'm poor in packets of Kool-Aid
I'm poor by the mark of my shoe
Not one but two talk when I walk
I'm poor by the amount of friends I keep
So by your eyes I'm bankrupt.
But let me tell you something
It's material things that make me bankrupt.
I'm really rich
Rich I tell you
Why I have a heart that's full of love.
I'm rich by the things you can't see.
It so full of love it raises my blood pressure.
So if you're counting digits I got none
Just put down 2-zero
Cut 'em in ½ and squeeze them together in the form of a heart
And that's how rich my Lord I follow
Made me—And you can
Bank on that baby!

-S.L.L.

HOME

Criminal/reject/damaged goods/monster
I am everything and I am nothing
In you I am reborn
You are my star that guides me
bring me out of darkness.
Flawed and Twisted, I will become
everything I have fought not to be.
The sun rises and shines in you
I will repent
You are my reason for being
In you I am HOME.

-L.B.

COFFEE WITH CLASS

It is called coffee with true class
and it's not my ass; it's his stash
comes in packs of eight, not ten
leaving pleasures through certain
measures. one cup = no cents (sense)
my heart then
breaks
without that
I'll never know
when to shut my legs
enjoying real taste

-K.M.R.

DAMAGED GOODS

Unable to look at you without tears running down my cheeks, snot dripping out my nose. Forty-eight years was a long time ago.

You were a beautiful little innocent child, a four-year-old princess wanting to love and be loved. How did he see you as sexy, desirable, and a turn-on?

Being the only girl, no sisters, no female cousins, no role model—it has been so alone. Too much time has been spent on blaming yourself. You were the child, he was the adult. Look at yourself now ... Forty-eight years from when it first started; it is still dictating your decisions and you are sitting in jail, looking at seven years in prison because you refused to be abused by another man, so you cut him. And it is all still causing tears to run down my cheeks, snot dripping out my nose.

p.s. I'm here for you.

-J.K.

UNTIL WE MEET AGAIN

Until we meet again
I promise to be the best Mother I can be
and make you proud of me.
Until we meet I will walk around and sing to you
like I used to when you were inside of me.
Until we meet again
Mommy and Daddy will Celebrate July 29th every year
as if you were here.
Until we meet again
baby boy
the whole world going to know about you.
Until we meet again
I will cherish every day you were growing inside of me
and the 19 hours of labor pain.
Until we meet again
I will never forget
the two hours they gave me to share with you.
Until we meet again
baby boy
you will always have a special place in my heart
and just know
Mommy can't wait
until we meet again

-J.H.

DEAREST OLYMPIA

Don't forget that you are amazing, because you are about to encounter so many haters, manipulators, negative influences and ulterior motives. The demure, kind-hearted, lady-like dove that your parents molded you to be is going to become a gregariously blazing phoenix rising from the flaming ashes a jaded, cold-hearted bitch.

Not that that's a bad thing. You are too nice, you give too much. So, don't be generous, save some for yourself. Make all of your mistakes loudly. Drink more SoCo. Stay that extra week in London, kiss your girlfriend before they send her away. Take no one's advice but your own. Keep listening to your mother. Bleach that mohawk platinum. Go to the Police about rape. Cheer 'til your voice gives out at your sister's ballgames. Eat more chocolate. Sing at the top of your lungs. Learn to curse quickly, to walk on your hands, to slow it down some.

If you decide to be who they want you to be, do what they want you to do, you might not end up being the life of the party. The one everybody watches, the original sage they turn to for guidance. And you certainly won't end up giving birth to a prince. You won't end up being ME. So keep kicking ass to the beat of the ten thousand drummers in your head. Continue to fear nothing. Stay regret free. Trade nothing for your journey. I sure won't.

P.S. Your destiny is greatness

Love,
An Incarcerated You

-O.J.

MY DEAREST BABIES' DADDY

These sticky-icky, dark, vinegary smelling feelings
they're coming out from my heart.
I can even feel the needle prick into my arm.
I'm alone in a cell because I was blinded by you.

I thought I was in love, but of course that wasn't true.
It started out with each of us in love with the same things:
a syringe, water, and cotton
and a number of mind and body numbing dreams

We didn't like being alone
with our hearts beating out feelings.
So resorted to Chiva, Roxies, Dilaudid, Smack, Morphine
a number of different things.

But then we met that cold, cold night.
Even though I knew something was off,
I never wanted to leave your sight.

You claimed you knew me and understood me
that you always will.
Then one thing led to another

We weren't dealing with only love
or just another pill.

-C.A

WHAT IT'S LIKE TO BE MARRIED TO A BAD COP

Most see black and white, me however, I see black and blue
More often than not—I spot a new shiner
With scars so deep—not just in my back—but on my heart
It looks as if I fought with Edward Scissorhands and sadly lost.

No DNA required—I know it's only my blood that is
Stained throughout the house.
I hear the siren and know what it must mean—sadly
Nothing more but a punchline to a bad joke
He knows they will not help me and laughs

I slowly peel away that badge—like it was a scab
From a bike wreck that never really healed
Revealing a monster that was never under my bed—but lying next to me.
In it.

"Freeze! Put your hands up!"
Never relaxing, you keep them up always, blocking punches.
"911, what's your emergency?"
That was never an option for me.
Only the neighbor who found me crumpled on the bathroom floor
After taking a steel-toed boot to my entire body, while hearing,
"Look at you. You're nothing. No one will ever love you."
But surviving to say he was so wrong.

-L.S.

WHAT IT'S LIKE TO BE OLD AND GAY

It's like Hell to be old and gay.
The condemnation, the laughter, the ridicule.
To me it's like fun and laughter and companionship.
To Hell what other people think.
They don't live my life for me.
They have no right to judge me, unless they want to be judged by God.
It's like their insecurity in their own lives makes them ridicule and mock and talk about me.
I am happy and content with myself.
It's like being a notch in the middle
of the Bible Belt

-J.S.

WHAT YOU WOULD FIND AT MY MOSSY CROSSROADS

The end of my ropes,
Candles burnt at both ends,
Buzzy Buzzing Orange Bees; hearts on
the mend...
Golden Quiet Sunrays, Chemical Fumes
Crystal shards, broken pipes, lighters,
rigs and spoons...
Praises to my Lord
thank for his Amazing Grace;
Laughter and hope, treasures of string,
Peacefulness, My lovers face...
Pages of wrong choices,
Plans to make it Right...
A lonely yoga mat and pants that fit
too tight...
3:00 p.m. naps to the Jazzy beat of
rattling keys, what ifs
A Compass pointing toward
a sanitary future, and A time
piece that skips.

-L.H.D.

HERE IN F-18, THE EXTENT OF MY LIFE

For the past seven months this pod has become the extent of my life.
Everything about this place has become too familiar. On my bunk, in my cell.
Parenting class, poetry and yoga, visitation, court holding, bible study and chapel are my only forms of escape/relief.

Breakfast, lunch and dinner, faces, bitches, brown trays, fifty shades of orange all smudged together. Doors buzz open, laughter, cursing, crying, chatter.

"Touch yourself, sista!" "Prayer Circle" "Lock Down!"
all blurred into white noise.
Females, armpits, socks, simple green, food cart smells,
all fill the air.
MAN, I can't *wait* to pull chain!

-S.G.H.

I FORGOT

Needle in your arm
Shackles on your wrists
"Oh, I forgot you was hard."

Babies wondering why
Husbands without a clue
"Oh, I forgot you was hard."

Another check lost
No money to be found
"Oh, I forgot you was hard."

The clock keeps ticking
Time is all gone
In a state of confusion
"You forgot you was hard"

-M.R.

DEAR JESSICA MARIE

The road you have walked down
has been real rough.
All the hurt and pain you have been through
to be so young
you are strong.
You are a very smart, outgoing young lady.
Girl, you have to be walking with angels to have made it this far.
The people God put in your life are for a reason.
God has a plan for you.
You have to be strong to lose two children and stay strong after all of that.
To lose the only man who ever loved you like the strong queen you are.
One day, someone is going to hug you so tight all your broken pieces
will stick back together again.

P.S. You have to love yourself.

-J.H.

HERE IN THE DUNGEON OF MY LIFE

The walls are thin, no longer a safe haven.
Yet I feel safe.
The floor is shallow but thick enough for no escape.
Time stands still with no justification for the things we talk about or do.
The yelling and screaming daily
making my ears ring like the slamming down of the phone receiver.
The cold of orange floating around as if there is no such thing as another color.
The salty taste of tears washing each eyeball away with wishes of going somewhere.
No guarantees, promises, or commitments happening, but each day another day closer.
Dreams dissipate with a new hope of a more colorful future.

-E.P.

HOPE

I need to wake up stand up.
It's a nightmare
It leaves me breathless
I feel like I'm going insane
Is it going to be forever?
Am I going down in flames?
It leaves me breathless
worry, doubt, fear
I'm scared, I'm drowning
Will I survive or am I going to die?
I try to speak but nothing comes out
It thinks its so real
so, please help me
it's time to change
it's time to make a difference
Please don't let me give up
or lose Hope

-M.M

WHAT YOU FIND IN PADEN, OK

Small rooms, dark skies, bright stars, million stars
Oil well pumping, scorpions in the tub, brown leather recliner, Prince Albert can
Yellow fingertips, rolling papers, soft hands, smell of Oil of Olay
Yeast rolls--mouth-watering-warm
One little girl, two proud parents of grand, one missing dad
Scrapbook, catalog paper dolls, Princess Diana magazine clippings
Antique jewelry, music box with a turning ballerina, fluffy homemade quilts
Learning to tie shoes, beautiful flower beds
Long walk to mailbox, riding shoulders on the way back
Piercing blue eyes of Paw Paw, soft skin of Maw Maw
Ready to go home to Mamma.

-A.R.N.

THIS PLACE

Upon my arrest, my world tilted off its axis
This place leaves me feeling something between
shock and disbelief
My life now consists of sleeping, eating, walking and reading day in and day out
All simple actions, requiring simple thoughts.
Just going through the motions
This place is cold and mechanical
and it's hindering my ability to
give a fuck.

-S.H.

THE STRUGGLE OF LIFE

For every struggle I'm transformed.
Kindness is a language the dumb can speak
and the deaf can hear. You are granted one measure of love
For every tear you brush from a cheek; I promise kindness
will follow, will flow. Wherever you walk, under
rainbows or stars over struggle, or down lonely hollows
I grant you one heart full of love and hope
For every smile you place on a face
I wish you two stars from above
The gift you earned from the lessons you learned
There is nothing the body may suffer that the soul can not accept.
In order to be a realist you must believe in miracles.
I am who I am when no words seem appropriate.

-K.H.

HANDS STORY

My hands have been through everything with me. They have been one thing that I can always trust and always count on. All the way from when I was a baby until now. My hands help me to explore things, pick them up , put them in my mouth. They helped me to crawl from one place to another. My hands helped me to grab hold of something and pull myself up. As time went on I learned to catch and throw things. One of my favorite things I learned was to blow my mom a kiss, and to catch hers, and save it in my pocket for later. When I was a teenager my hands became stronger. I worked every day, from sun up to sun down. As the time came, I used my hands to defend myself and they became my weapons to survive. Though the darkness of those times was the beginning of my destruction, the fighting became a way of life. It turned into loading a pipe, to blowing a pipe, to rolling a pipe, ten and two, ten and two. It almost cost me my life and about lost my hand. To where I am today, I use my hands to wipe tears, help pick another up and to praise and worship my God.

-M.M.

AN ODE TO THIS OLD JAIL

No matter how I feel
I am still in jail
I can't rest at all
I am sighing and sobbing
I don't want to be here at all
My cell is gloomy
My bed is hard
My spirit is crying
I have nothing at all
Guards are all rude, they are such brutes
Could it be that I am tattooed or because I am feeling blue?
I'm tired of these chains
I just need a damn key
They took away my pride
I sit here powerless
It's raping my soul
Jailhouse food restricts my bowels
I sit on the toilet and howl
Wonder how I got here and how I'm gonna get out...
Poor jail bird trapped in her cage.
The voices all echo, it's maddening my brain
I'm doing time
time, time time
I am now the beholder of time
My journey is long, my time is so slow
I feel so old

-Anonymous

WHAT IT'S LIKE TO BE SO FAR AWAY (FOR THOSE OF YOU WHO AREN'T)
Translated from Spanish

A different country.
They don't know me.
It's like feeling not protected
I'm trying to be happy but my eyes reflect the sadness that I carry.
It's like hypocrisy.
I miss my parents and I want to embrace them
and I feel that solitude/aloneness.
It's as if I'm cold and I'm not cold.
Every moment every day lost without the love of my life
--for wanting to achieve a dream that has turned into a nightmare.

-C.R.

WHAT YOU WILL FIND UNDER MY COVER

Clean needles for the next shot/no lighter to heat the spoon/broken pipes and dirty cotton/skin burning" and crawlin' because I missed a shot. Who would have known that I'd break another heart just to get that high we chase. Vroom, vroom, casino here I come! Ready to get that good old fix/hopin' and praying the dealer I meet has just the right amount for me. Oh, we all have a problem, we're all addicts. It just seems to be that *meth* became the fucking drug for me.

-G.D.

WHY

Why do we stay
Once the love is gone?
Why am I afraid of being alone?
No one to hold
No one to lean on
Where the hell has it gone?
Why the hell has he gone?
My Love is lost like the petals of a summer rose
Maybe my Love will come back to me
Why do we stay and wait?
What am I waiting on?
Why has he forsaken me?
You took up all my time and space.
You demolished my Dreams.
You Raped my passions.
So why do I keep holding on?
Oh, why do I wait.

-D.C.

WHAT IT'S LIKE--PRISON LIFE (FOR THOSE OF YOU WHO DON'T KNOW)

It's waiting on a letter when you're doing time.
Family won't write or send you a dime.
It's waiting on visits that never take place.
Friends and family who forget your face.
It's hearing them lie, saying they'll try.
It's making plans with someone
but plans change and they don't include you.
It's hearing how much they care
but in your time of need they are never there
It's hearing their promises go straight to your head
but when push comes to shove they'll leave you for dead.
It's feelings of love, honor and pride
pain and emotions, hurting inside.

-Anonymous

UNTITLED

Once upon a time, a little brown skinned girl was created...
by God...
carrying a Basket of Love in my hands.
She was given no special tools to use
or distribute
this Love.
Only her human hands.
Early childhood, these hands of mine dressed my dolls and combed their hair...
Oh so skillfully...
As a young adult, these hands of mine distributed lotion to babies' bottoms
School lunches for lunch pails
and wrapped many a Christmas gifts.
Yes, these!
Hands created to distribute from this Basket of Love.
And, now!
These hands may appear
to be a little wrinkled to the world
But, I still have that
Basket of Love
and these hands that care!

-C.A.

LOCKDOWN

There are sixty seconds in a minute
Sixty minutes in an hour
Lockdown.

Being confined to a room makes it hard to see the moon
the stars in the sky
and you ask me why
I'm looking dark with gloom.

Slow and pain free
What time is it? Can you see?
It's lockdown time.

Doing time in jail
being locked down on lockdown in lockdown is Hell.

Lockdown done in two minutes
Welcome to Jail.

-L.J.H.

ODE TO INDIGENT ENVELOPES

Envelopes big and small
they come in handy
and we don't have many at all.
Some sell them for noodles
and some trade noodles for them.
They only come monthly
so use them with care
otherwise your locker will soon turn up bare.

-E.P

WHAT IT'S LIKE TO BE ME

I'm lyrical. I'm spiritual. I'm a hopeful soul that believes in miracles. I'm a masked prisoner, the judge was my sentencer. Do you wanna talk about you? Cause I'm a good listener. I'm a lonely stoner. Never a condoner. I'm an agonized groaner. A midnight love-making-moaner. I'm a lover. Not a fighter. I'm a struggler. But I'm a survivor. I'm a 1, 2, piece, good-nighter. I never jump out of the car, cause I'm a rider. I can't stand a liar. I keep it real. Bluntness is my weakness. I can't help but to tell you how I really feel. Blame it on my A.D.D. - I can't stand still. I'm down with the sickness. I ain't ill I don't miss a meal. I'm a fat girl. I blame my problems on 2014's world. Did I mention I'm A.D.D. - Ball. Car. Squirrel. I live to die. And I'll die when I live. I'm bisexual, but at the moment, I'm anti-men. I sin. My name's Danielle. God is my judge and there's not a soul that's bigger than Him. Can I get an Amen? At times I win and at times I lose. I've loved and lost, but that's the cost when I've been torn and broken and my body and soul has suffered severe abuse. When I love... I love BIG. And I have a big heart. So.. I have plenty of love to give. But careful- Don't take advantage of it. Cause one time, shame on you. And two times, shame on me. I learn from my mistakes. My company leaves me no misery. Believe you, me, I'm a defiant rebel. All about that bass, no treble. I'm a naughty Catholic girl. I rebuke the devil. You'll never see me eye to eye 'til you get on my level. I believe in the stars, fate, hope, and destiny. My dearest "anam caras"... translation- "soul friends"... Poetic Justice is what it's like to be me.

-D.H.

THE LOVE OR DRUGS

Love is like a drug you really can never get enough of.
It's like fire running through your veins and all the lil' rushing things.
Love can come and go so fast
all you want is to make it last
but with the drugs there is no love because you have lost all your trust.
You begin to steal
maybe even kill
but most of all it's for the thrill.
So you hate instead of love because you've chosen that fucking drug
the drug that went into your vein
that nearly drove you insane.
You begin to drift
and even forget about the love you almost missed.
So open your eyes and do it fast
and put that shit in your past.
Throw the needle to the ground
and tell ol' dude to move around
cause he could have missed
and you would have been pissed.
So just love instead of doing drugs
and maybe then we could gain some trust.

-C.T.

PANTIES SOMEONE ALREADY WORE

The butt-crack of dawn
I sleepwalk along
in panties
someone else
wore before me

I stand in a line
smells like bad breath and ass
for orange grits and maybe some meat
then back to sleep
for a few pleasant dreams

wake up to the echoes
"You stupid bitch"
It's time to start the day

I shuffle along as new D.O.'s shuffle
I laugh, I cry, I sing

I wait for the trays
fight off the strays
and pray to God we don't get
ahem...

Then dinner comes on
this day almost gone
it's Alpo again
with no sauce

Eight days and a shackle
no more Michelle's
no more noodles
Goodbye to David L. Moss!

-S.P.

WHAT IT'S LIKE TO BE SCARRED AND PRETTY

It's like looking in a mirror not knowing who you see.
It's like there is something missing.
Who is staring back at me?
It's like each scar represents a self-made puzzle piece.
It's like I don't know who I am until I start to bleed.
It's like the scars get deeper with every year.
It's like shattering that mirror and craving the sharpest piece.
It's like going through this life, not knowing how to feel.
It's like going through this life, not knowing how to deal.
It's like being scarred and pretty is the only way to heal.

-L.B.

ODE TO BEAUTY

Oh my gosh!
A place that eventually shows your natural skin, eyes, facial flaws and all,
The picture that is taken of what you looked like before, it all gets washed off.
The tremendous looks, questions on the females' faces...
My first response is ask me no questions, I tell you no lies.

We all look different with flaws and all.
The braids, orange outfits, style of individuals.
The colored pencils as makeup starts to draw a sense of beauty for us all.

I can't wait to get out and apply Mac, Estee Lauder, lashes, contacts, extensions,   hair
color, botox, laser hair removal...
Hell, look like Sofia Vergara - the goddess of all!
Heels, Gucci, Fendi, Versace, any and all
Just want to be the beauty that we all deserve to be.

The beauty is you, all that we know we have.
Flawless, finesse let's strut it all.
You and I are beautiful inside and out.
Oh my gosh, I never would have imagined.
You got it girl, work it like Barbie
just don't fall.

-P.L.

UNTITLED

New Year, New Life
choices change
I am a free bird caged!

-C.P.

BEAUTIFUL TWEAKER

What was it like to be a tweaker?
It was like staying up all night while looking good
Now ain't that right?
It was like being everywhere and trying to get there on time
Like fidgeting of the hands--worried about your man
Or grinding of the teeth
Up all night roaming the streets
With not an appetite to eat
Just the streets and staying tweaked
to see how many tasks you could complete.

-C.T.

ODE TO BEING CAUGHT (THE END: GAME OVER)

Head spinning
Worried about everything
Scared to look my family in the eye.
Ashamed I relapsed after eight years clean.
In only one year
Lost what I gained.
Happy and excited the law caught up to me
Now I can breathe.
I'm behind bars but can look my mom straight in the eyes during visitation.
Only a little worried about what my consequence will be.
Ready to go back out there and show my boys what a wonderful life we can have.
Thank God for The End.
Game Over.

-S.O.

WHAT IT'S LIKE TO BE A FLAMBOYANTLY GAY LATINO MAN TRAPPED INSIDE A SARDONIC BLACK WOMAN'S BODY (FOR THOSE OF YOU WHO AREN'T)

It's wanting to wear day glo yellow and pink
but knowing it does not flatter my skin tone.
It's wanting to fly to Fire Island for a week
but knowing it's better to stay at home
and be a good mother to my son.
It's loving Barbra Streisand, Gloria Estefan,
Bette Midler, Sandra Bernhardt.
It's the desire to walk into a "black" church
without feeling like I'll be struck by lightning.
It's sashaying, it's Cosmos, it's high heels
It's the strut-strut-turn that I picked up from Drag Queens.
It's telling my son to leave the room while I watch
Ru Paul's "Drag Race" on Tuesdays
It's having strapping thighs that don't jiggle
but a bouncy ass with just enough wiggle.
It's loving sexy men
It's hating sexy men, but having sex with them anyway.
It's personifying the pliability of hormonal enigma.
It's exuding salacious, sweet, sticky sensuality.
It's being stuck between a rock and an exceedingly hard, swinging paced place
and loving every rhythmically abrasive minute of it,
damn it.
Mostly, it's never being seen for the truest me
and never really desiring to be.

-O.J.

WHAT IT'S LIKE TO BE A MOTHER

It's like sunshine sometimes
It's a wonderful melody
at times it's painful to hear
It's like a bad storm that roars loudly
It's gentle, soft, soothing rain, through the tears.
It's beautiful music with different notes and sounds
soft tones high and low
It's the most enchanting dance you'll ever dance.

-D.C.

UNTITLED

One bully, two bully, three bully four,
Naughty and never nice you will
Find behind alphabetized doors.
A "yard" looking through a window
You see each in orange fake smiles, broken hearts,
To them we are nothing but a bunch of ants in a cage
With nothing to explore.
Clicking locked.
Buzzed unlocked.
Eight ordinary gray tables.
No nights
Too many wanna-be-queens
Grey sidewalk, grey carpet, grey chairs, grey everywhere
Even in the air.
Black and white you don't see unless in the fine print
When you sign away your life with your written consent.
Camera one.
Camera two.
Always criticizing the good. Never watching the bad
Like they should.
Duct tape and super glue.
Nope. Not here.
Toothpaste and Bob Barker soap is what will do.
Pink towel.
Pink washcloth.
White tile squares with grey dots
Not big enough for hopscotch.
Among the orange a few stand out.
Fed Red. Do it big or not at all.
At least that's what they said
Remember the Brady Bunch?
Marsha, Marsh, Marsh, not quite,
Mersa, Mersa, Mersa, a bacteria with a painful bite!
T.V. to the left, one to the right
Yet no one will agree what's on tonight.

Level 1 and 2 be on lock down
Level 3 and 4 get to move around.
I could go on and on but honestly
I just wanna close my eyes till I hear my freedom song.

-Anonymous

FOR MORE INFORMATION

FOLLOW US ON FACEBOOK AT:
Poetic Justice Oklahoma

FIND US AT:
www.OLAA.org

EMAIL US AT:
PoeticJusticeOKLA@gmail.com